T0363742

Wystan's Relic

Shaun Berg was born in Adelaide, Australia in 1967. His undergraduate studies were at the University of Adelaide. He has travelled widely throughout his life. He lives in South Australia.

Wystan's Relic

Shaun Berg

**Wakefield
Press**

Wakefield Press
1 The Parade West
Kent Town
South Australia 5067
www.wakefieldpress.com.au

First published 2013

ISBN 9 781 74305 293 8

Front cover design by Peta Astbury
Typeset by Wakefield Press
Printed in Australia by Prestige Copying and Printing, Adelaide

For reading, not reciting

Contents

1. The Dead of War

The cops and robbers together,
scale the towers of the walled city
and roam among the living.
Their nightmare dreams
blemish the stars, and for a time,
the captured dreamers
outnumber the fugitives.

Death does not rage upon me
but caresses my brow
and encourages
a deep rolling sleep.
Seductively compelled,
I departed this world of dwarves.
My cries released the angels
delusion pounds the pavement,
and the news from the grave
lay end to end.

My existence had fooled itself
into meaning, but, for me,
every hand had grabbed
for the sword, and the vicious beast,
however badly,
muddled the mirrors, always.
The dead of war
embarrass the myth
of human conscience.

2. Our Descent into Spoil

For a moment
the silence respects
the unsuspecting landscape.
But then, a dozen hoods
position their siege guns
and rain bombs from the sky.
The plumes of their madness
rise periodically
from the killing fields.

In nature,
the absence of malice
makes demands
for innocence
in every place.
But still the envies
march upon
the scholar's name
and pledge allegiance
to the stains.

The watchers creep
along the shore
among the dandelions.
The vices of this crisis
lay ankle deep
in tasteless bread.
The sour wine sinks into
small complaint.

In another day
of ordinary destiny
the best years of our lives
are razed to the ground.
Every decency rages
and from opposite banks
we mark our descent into spoil.

In this ditch of hopeless odds,
no man can persevere;
ignorance and innocence
remain divided
by desire.

3. The Ugly Life of the Rejected

When he closes his eyes
for that last time
his last glimpse of life
is of unruliness, and theatre.
He thinks to himself,
no doubt many will be jealous
of my death, and despise
my untimely exit.

For him, this cruellest hour
had other lives to live.
No longer did the injured
lead the ugly life
of the rejected.
No longer did false regret
stand reciting the past
in the present.

He retreated from reason
on a rocking horse,
and remained consumed
by the misery of habit.
He did not choose life
but once alive
he improved himself
on too few occasions
by living.

4. The Loss of Ruined Awakenings

The shy hands
bravely confront
the mysteries behind
the single note.
Each remains locked
in the recesses
of the loving shade.
Each crime
to the earth
mocks the corroding keys,
and silences
the tired language
of the shocked prophets.

The sun sets
upon the valley
of the foxes.
The chance to weep
for the crimson soldiers
belies the error
of the robber's heart.
Fickle time
has tired of this torrent
of language,
it drifts along
the flooded brook.

Long in the distance
the love does rejoice.
But lies and trickery,
the conditions of the heart,
fall lightly upon the earth.
Silence sets down, upon
the agreeable woods.

Still the captors
are buried
as faithful servants
in a hunting ground
of broken bones.
With deep emotions
the fool grieves
the tattered loss
of ruined awakenings.

5. The Sanctuary of the Absurd

Shaken by the gentle wind
he was prompted
to seek the truth.
He hurries among
the stones looking
to the features
of human folly.

Distracted by the children
dying in the streets
he seeks relief
in the sanctuary
of the absurd.
He accuses the leopard
of being a childish creature.

His fear of the truth
pushes him to madness.
His muttered utterances
breed the locust
and they devour
the earth
piece by piece.
Unaware of the menace
blissfully, the others
remained drawn to magic.

Many
in their ordinary days
are oblivious
to their doom;
they dream of love and hate.
Human weakness
has greatest capacity
to wreak the soul.

6. The Deserted Hearts

In the trance of time abyss
the boy inherits
the outworn images
of the dead.
But for him,
never did the sorrow
last forever;
over time
it became the margins
then the distance, and
the dancing stranger.

The silent breath
in the dark woods
is no longer tolerated;
he retreats,
from the perfect calm.
Expectedly, the roses convalesce
near the shores of the deserted
hearts; they are blessed
among the trembling
fortresses.

He willingly
would give
the lightness to the darkness
for his twilight dreams.
He still weeps
for the lives
his wishes, never lived.
Then, like the pieces
of a broken vase
he embraces the universe.

In his last moment,
adding insult to injury,
the starless night
steals a kiss
from the moonlight;
and the false heart
bribes the mirror
with its own reflection.

7. The Plans of a Thief

In every garden, scarecrow prophets
throw coins into the wishing well
and deliver, their necks
to the grateful sword.
The unwise madman
continues to crawl
through the lilac bushes, searching
for the earth's daughter.

He takes independent delight
in the perception
of the isolated lark;
the mad and the ill.
Little does he know
that even the rats
have deserted the causes.
He makes the plans of a thief
and watches the night anxiously
counting the days.

By late afternoon
the warped melodrama of the day
has made the necessary errors
and in his failure, like huddled corpses,
his goodness is wasted.
Along with the fate of ships
all men consider marginal grief
the cornerstone of life.

8. The Victim's Heart

The frost escapes
the humbled misery
of this isolated place.
Misadventure obscures
and the assembled histories
become etched
onto the stranger's face.
In the city squares
the wanderers
of the cold streets
shake off winters' hold.

Near the tangled fountain
a lifetime of flesh and bones
emerges, in the shape of a man.
As he pushes his way
through age to death
another of his type, glances
the menacing notices
of the daily newspaper
and yet another catches a boy
falling from the sky.

Night after night
these lonely
battered lives regret
their temporary moments
of living.
Left wanting
for the miracles
of spring's compulsion
each waits,
for the happenings.

Meanwhile,
the innocent offenders
betray the victim's heart
with their offence
and the invisible furies
living a lifetime of hatred
kneel to pray.

9. To the Darkness we Exit

To snipe at the painter's inspiration
to destroy the image of the breach
to stride across the barren worlds;
deftly the foul stench of the monsters
impress upon the frightened miracles.

The burn victims come to drink the cool waters.
They wish for their desires and their faded memories.
Appreciation breaks the interest of the tempest with
    frail insincerity.
The earth flounders until the flesh forgives the
    moment's journey.

The memories spin around like an empty box
the clouds continue to hang over the huge crowds
the gaunt and the famed, blush;
the violation of every interest continues.

As the sufferers continue to suffer
the watchers put their questions to the answers.
The period of light flickers too soon;
from the darkness we enter, to the darkness we exit.
In the short moments of existence, do not let the last
    hour pass;
for there is no decency in entering every heaven.

10. Through the Eyes of a Dreamer

The stone dogs
guard the privacy
of the hollowed man.
As the ills of fortune demand,
his voice
finds a hearing
in the paradox of time.
He speaks to others
in an atlas
of tongues.

He is the ace of spades
reversed.
His betrayal is rooted, in the tricks
of his generation
each ably following
the rash performances
of the long dead.

Time watches him
tie his shoe laces
the breeze washes over
his fake journey
the dull spirited flowers
remains hungry
for the friendless sun;
the slave refuses to break,
and the victim, lies awake, wary
of the shrewd tomorrow.

As he becomes weaker
than his thoughts
the illnesses
of the living, overcome him,
the miracle he awaits,
never happens
and the furies
are assigned,
to the destiny
of the victim's heart.

There is nothing left
for the wishing well
but to rediscover life
through the eyes
of the dreamer.

11. The Fancy of Every Riddle

Regardless
how baseless
the ruined faces
the boxwood hedge
is evidence
that the universe
lies shattered
and shaken by
the shrieking nymphs.
The dogs
of these days
are limp
and dead.

In the tired town
the sleeping man
grasps
his own conditions.
He prays knowledge
will find him, but it justifies
only the doubts
in his mind
and the absurd
are left alone
to despair
at each turn.
A maze
has no plan
able to gratify
the human heart; and
the perfect corner
is the fancy
of every riddle.

Gossip, spite,
the almost true
sits quietly, waiting,
for the matters
blurred.
The soothing shores
fluent and seamless
remain content;
blue is
my favourite lilac.

12. My Spring of Delicate Yellow

The dogs
bark in the dark
the local people
price the flowers
in the valley; among them
a shapeless figure
sits on a bench.
This man wears
an indistinguishable hat
and thinks of nothing.
I talk at him
until his teeth
chatter.

Nearby,
I notice blood splattered
on the public gardens.
It was,
the keenest sign
of life I had seen
in this dead heart town.
This was my spring
of delicate yellow.

Still
my penniless
injured eyes
saw only
the sad envies.
The reckless
are blessed
for they do not care
at what angle
they are regarded.
But I am
the inconstant beast
that repeats
itself.

In this topsy-turvy world
my conduct is entirely predictable,
the keys that open
are the keys that rust.
In the flicker
of an eye
the robin vanishes
the raven enters
the orange grove
and the frogs
are drowned.

The poison
flows over
their folly
and horror.
Alone
through this sewer I walk.
Somewhere
in a magical
evening gown
the prostitute
lays down
with her
imaginary friend.

13. The Longer are my Days

The tragic wanderer
in this world of menace
locates his conscious
amongst the dust
and the stones.
The ordered mayhem
of his existence
remains lost
to the lunatic's agitation.
The stones
ruthlessly mock
and embarrass him.

With no mortal distractions
the wanderer invites
the dust to support his soul.
In a mere puff of eternity
the dust cracks the silence
and the tortured soul floats
through unfractured time.

Undead now
he is detached
from his frivolous existence
his features gone.
Unabashed by context
free from reason
and memory
friendship or love;
the disharmony of life
is replaced
by the confidence
of belief
his ego is shredded
of pretence.

The divine power
is no longer mediated
through the foibles
of existence
and the tragic wanderer
reflects;
the longer
are the end of my days,
but no grander.

14. The Spirit of Mockery

He renders people
as characters,
as human beings,
emotionally unfolding,
passionately ambivalent
about their lovers;
they strive to find a rainbow;
they live in constant fear
that happiness, may be lost.
This cannot be true
it is insufferable
careless
repetitious,
fleshless,
intolerable;
the only consolation in the mire,
is my deference
to your intimacy.

Struggling
with feeling and desires,
existing
on the margins of life
unhappy with the privileges,
the prophet of the working classes,
that excruciating being,
remains madly driven
and chaotic.

It is pompous, impenetrable,
you are asked
to think
to correct
your imagination
to make it
what it is not;
this is a lie
in the spirit
of mockery.

I too
recognize love;
and death
does assist me
to overcome
my fears,
but, the crumbling
dissolution
of life
is a nonsense metaphor;
all things live
in inconstant sobriety;
sometimes
a little drunk
sometimes
a little confused.

Accomplished
and elegant
a magical realism
will survive;
every tiger
wishes
to falls in love.

15. The Weeping Clown

Through
this pen
all manner
of lies, come;
not that
every pusher
will be judged
by them.
By their gift
they can distance
their debauched lives
from the ideal
presentation
of their lives
lived.

As their vanity calls,
they enjoin
the ordinary life
of the treacherous clerk
and gardener.
The real,
never meets
the ideal
the reflection
never meets
the reflected;
apart and alone
they must live.

We can never think
of the moment,
or capture
its essence
in any other moment,
our thoughts
our intellect
can never analyse
the only meeting
that we are able
to know;
this is
the dilemma
that binds
us all.

The
weeping clown,
stumbles into
the dank parlour
of the fortune teller,
and the wind
returns
from where it
began.

16. A Child of the Times

The madness
was based
on the distinction
between
life
that was worthy
and life
that was unworthy;
'we are
the chosen ones',
they said,
'they are
our misfortunes'.

Cruelty
was rewarded;
that was
the mechanism
of their evil;
but
we all knew
they were
nothing
without
their uniforms.

Within,
they saw themselves
as the embodiment
of supermen,
capable of anything
even
the unthinkable
even
the unspeakable.

What a time
it was,
when a man
thought,
he could
achieve
acclaim and status
with pictures
like these.
It was an era
of undreamt
prospects,
from clerk
to general
in a moment.

He was
an educated man
who lived
without remorse.
He carried
out his orders
well.
He administered
the genocide
from his desk,
but in the end
the truth
caught up to him.

The lucky victims
bore witness
to his crimes:
'I dispute
the charges;
I never
beat a woman,
I was a child
of my times;
discipline
and loyalty
has bought me
to these gallows,
I put
my oar in
whenever
I could'.

No doubt
his children
when they clasp
their little hands
together to pray;
pray for god
to care
for father.

17. An Existence of Crooked Inches

This town
is nothing,
it is
a nothing town;
consumed
by unremarkable
actions,
and fashionable
madmen.
This is
the place
we live
and die.

The doomed man
dreams
of the affection
of the dead.
He cries
for the wanderers
and the lovers.
His possessions exist
only in
the noise and haste
of his busy griefs.

We are
the accused;
without spite
we accept
no fairer charge
has been laid.
He is tormented
to despair;
he survives
on a diet of rats
and lives
an existence
of crooked inches.

In life
as in death
the river
overflows
with tears
its heart
broken,
by the fickle
jade;
by the lingering
doubts.
He asks;
is there
no compensation
for the loss
of happiness.

18. Another Comic Role

The slave
distressed
by the accusations
refuses
the silent movements
of the well tailored
suit.
In this strange
tomorrow
he suspects,
the sleep
he craves,
will be traded
for another
comic role.

From this moment
he dominates
the peaceful skies
in the knowledge
the inevitable war
will continue
between
nature and foe.
The waste hints
at bleak hospitals
and virtues forbidden.

The foolish man
considers the pieces
torn from the clocks.
His insatiable hunger
will be satisfied only,
with his feasting
upon his own corpse.

19. In the Poisonous Night

Let the dead
bury their dead
under the floorboards
of the madhouse.
Make them fear
the violent cries
of their monster dreams.

Have them face
the unhinged creatures
screaming death scares
in the poisonous night.
Impose shackles
on their empty minds
and fear the rage;
for their souls
confront
the dying day.

20. For the Wants of Yesterday

I pulverize these monsters with my fists
I fight them with temper and tricks
from each pore, kindly
their bones, disjoin,
their past evaporates
into an ill-tempered scene.
Both naked and in nakedness
the known and the knowing
are shameless and ashamed.

The darkness opposes the spark
the music trips across the frozen lake
the rocks praise the craters
and the greenness refreshes the water lilies.
In this state the appropriation of grief
the silencing of mourners
warrants no critique of the politic.
It is the disappointment of man.
Far from this blessed sky
the mouth of the babe
releases a cry for the wants of yesterday.
Its scent, anxious and odd
is provoked, it is apathetic, storm beaten.

Without feelings a person
becomes lonely and alone.
No more can we cope
with the every days of our lives.
In the manner of the young
each prophecy
shall lie wrecked
under the ocean.
It is in the making and the giving.

21. Pools of Silence and Despair

More the pity lies;
entombed among the filth,
as such, the fool seeks to join
the ranks of the poets.
But by his weak character
he becomes estranged
from the integrity of his gift.

Doubt and uncertainty
invade his existence;
regret divides reason
and his fractured heart
is weakened.
He stores his tears
amongst the photographs
of his innocent life.

Left by his friends
to dine with the demons
he weeps.
He concedes defeat
to the dogs.
For him
there is no solace
to be found in the rain
and the flowers.

Guided by tears
the fool reaches
into his heart.
He finds nothing,
the depth of his childhood
are pools of silence
and despair.

22. The Sanctuary of their Heaven

Blossom and grace
have modified the earth.
They mourn
the lost memory
of the childlike expression.
Weeping flowers
drift in the dust
of these petty tremors.

No more
is the sword
taken to the garden.
Love grows
among the stones
it roots pit
deep into the earth.
Shapes are their own genius.

Madness is interrupted
the shepherd breathes
more easily on the hill.
Racked by pain
all men detest
the sanctuary
of their heaven.

Some among them
recognise regret
as the faultless myth
never understood.
Most insist
that evil is love
denied them.
The importance
of tomorrow
is given over to the raw isolation
that begets the deserted hearts.

23. All These Tears

I remember
her first words to me
on that last morning.
In a determined whisper she said,
'I wish to die'.

As those words
were released from her
I recognized there was
no way to resist them.
It was at that time
my own resolve evaporated
and she slipped quietly away.

Nobody stood over me
watching my grief,
no record was made
of its intensity,
but for all these tears
nothing existed.

All that remains now
are my feelings of loss;
existing in another dimension,
in another place
beyond everything
but myself.

These feelings,
they influence nothing,
for others
they are nothing
they are my own;
in this complex world
they are my existence.

24. The Art of Self-Forgetting

I always considered it art
nothing more.
It was a friend
heartfelt;
it was a deep romance;
equivalent
to a dream.

When you get close to perfection, he said
the pain is constant;
I feel it is something to be expected;
hurting is art.

Refrain from the slow train
keep away from
the wasted crazy streets,
at their best they can only
dement you.

I think everything
is possible;
nothing is fixed
not until the last drop of paint
touches the canvas.

Reaching the summit
for me, only converted
my loss to yearning.
It became a mere numbness;
brazen and comical, listless,
beyond the extreme.

This overarching ambition
monumental in itself
enthralled me it made me
an unstoppable hurricane;
the pattern of things
was set
from the start.

I began to dig down into the earth.
After some time, sometime,
after I began digging,
I felt stunned
and exhausted,
dead to myself;
I became self forgetting.

25. The Ghosts of the Forest

The deep sobs
from the sobbing child
humiliates the clown.
He lay prostrate
on the ground
gripped by the fear
of more sobs
each inflicting
greater hurt and pain
upon him
than the last.

He is too empty to fight
to struggle against
the awfulness
of it all,
he closes his eyes
and gives way
to the ghosts
of the forest.

He is alone, his soul
seeks another vessel,
this one,
that has served
him dear,
is empty now.

The deaf girl weeps
for this death,
the snare
is forgotten and
the bee again
feels drawn
to the flower.

26. The Delight of Every Madman

Unearthed
in the earthen jars
the caresses
buried
by the loving shade
find peace
among the beggar's memories.
The numbness
acts oddly,
having escaped
the dissent
of the broken laws;
the delight of every madman
remains the same;
their end routine.
Meanwhile
the lepers
indulge
in the detail
and routine
of their robbers' burning.
Retreating
from the earth
they shrink
from the panic
and cry
in the silence alone;
for the love
and affection
of their vices;
nearby,
opportunity weeps.
The errors
of youth
shall meet
too many crimes.

27. He Painted Mountains

It was not a pleasant time in his life.
Everything else but his work was irrelevant.
Even his friends needed to make an appointment
to see him through his lawyer.

I think it was he hated his mother,
but I do not mean that in a Freudian sense;
I mean that, he packed up his grief and joy,
and left the place where she lived.

He liked to keep every relationship,
every strand of his life, separate.
Something would excite him,
and that would be his inspiration.

I have never been that keen
on happy endings, he once said to me.
In his life, he said, he had become unhappy
so he retired to paint mountains.

I asked him to explain this to me.
He said, 'I believe that lakes were built,
for swans to float on and all I have done
in my life is to proceed to drain those lakes'.
I am left tormented now in my life,
to duel with my own shadow
every aspect of my conduct, predicted.

28. My Childhood

A lucky few had seen it through the life of a child.
For me, it was bad news, just bad news.
A misfortune that was undeserved, isolating and
    incredulous.
It was a scandal that could bring down a career,
but of course, that was when I wanted a career.
It pushed me into a quiet corner.
I was left to ponder myself, and wrest, with my
    monsters.

Outside, I overcame, what was an extremely traumatic
    event, in my life.
When I was a child, a child was stolen, from the hope of
    its parents.
Its body was left to cry in the woods.
This happening made me feel entirely vulnerable.
My obsession, my madness, resulting, caused an
    enormous crisis in our family.
I was told firmly, it is not true, it did not happened.
But, it was etched into my brain, and once there, it was
    impossible to erase.
Only years, many years later, did I find out by chance,
    that what I knew was true.
It affected me deeply.

I knew also of the death of another child.
I threw a ball in a narrow hall way with a friend, it ran
    through him.
It bounced out of the building onto a road.
My friend chased it and was killed by a passing car.
I found a hole and I recoiled into it. But his mother
    found me.
Gently and forgivingly, she forgave me. This was my
    childhood.

Lost, and without my own childhood, I was unable to
  recognize another's.
I think it was for this reason I could speak truthfully,
  directly, and plainly to children.
I was a butterfly in a bell jar.

29. A Commonplace Encounter

It started a strange day. I awoke
with an unusual deliberateness.
I decided to build a bridge
from the middle of the river.

I desired, by my own hands,
to give something beautiful
to the world. I could wait
no longer to embrace this destiny.

I knew I existed
at most, ten minutes ahead
at best, ten minutes behind.
I began and I finished.

For a time, all I heard
was the monotonous sound,
of a cracked kettle. My product
was flinty, careless, and carefree.
It resembled a remembered postcard
of some depressive hamlet. It was
a common place encounter.

From these experiences, I know
the unexamined life craves intellectual
disintegration; self-knowledge,
is invariably, unsettling.

30. What Poetry Remains

The trees sleep
with the raging heart
of love lost.
The night birds
silently
trace their lives
from injured
to rejected
from frustration
to collapse.
The still night
humbles the constant stream
and the river recites
what poetry remains.

No man
exists on this earth;
the princes have fallen.
Their utterances
their dishonest mood,
their captured souls
are each now, the fancy of another place.
The discomfort
is part of
the anxious silence.

31. So Completely Alone

The tears of tomorrow
fall deliberately
onto the marble floor.
The memories of yesterday
distort.
These tears from heaven
make nothing of the tedium
of the day.

The slow tacit movement
of the beast
is resisted
for the horrors
existing
in every moment.
It manifest
as the demise
of the times.

The shoes
are filled
by the like minded.
They fall
into the nowhere
of tomorrow;
leaving depressed
the hoping.
There is no redemption
from the forest.
We are all
so completely
alone.

The forbidden
hinting
of a dark countryside
remains,
the glance
of a lover's compulsion.

32. An Ordered Life

The distraction
of the forces
of no moment
forever stop
the traveller's journey.
He cannot
bear the safety
of this existence
thrust upon him
by a fear
of grimaced
order.
It will grind
him slowly
inevitably
into
a finer grain
of dust.

He is not
as terrified
of death
as to deny
nature's natural end.
But he will not
let the black dogs
strip the bark
from this life.
To leave
its wasting genius
littered along
the track
with his love's
imagination.

He will haunt
the urinals
for a miracle
to embrace
a more clumsy life.

The god
of lesser men
will continue
to howl
at their
powerlessness;
the epitaph
of their humiliated will
has been degraded
by an ordered life
warped by
broken mirrors
reflecting a world
of nothingness;
it will cast
no shadow.

For the sake
of his own failings,
he honours the fate
of the dead,
and regrets forever
their demise.

33. An Unrelenting Business

I am alone with my thoughts, my troubles, my
    griefs.
I hope my hopes of something implausible;
the next page of an existence less ordinary,
even mildly, uneventful troubles; then alone
to quietly disappear to defeat.

I defy this small town; its misery defies me.
It dooms me to my own making;
life is an unrelenting business.
My grief dulls from green to grey to blue.
I rush to save nothing.

No happy ending comes to this mad plot
I continue my desperate struggle to despair.
Once reached, time gives me no warning of its
    patience lost.
In my humility I seek no contentment from it.
Rested, the edges of my mind dissolve.

34. A Tragedy of Goodness

As he enters the maze
he knows it has no plans
that can gratify his heart.
'I have so many words' he says
as he unites his fears in a single cut.
Like all others to be known,
this man believes, he creates
his own conditions.

But even the enlightenment
is safely criticized as a tragedy of goodness.
Pretty pieces of nonsense
are the only evidence of its remains.
To the imagination of the stones
the clouds exist to mirror each passing beauty
and the dirty snow leaves
the marble tombs to defend the whiteness.

Each image that can exist
is left to parade past the causes
and after a while the errors multiply.
Lost of their uniqueness for all time
this novelty comes to an end.
With fetters upon their souls
the unaware reminds us
that the world is a still pond
in which innocence drowns.

35. In Search of a Violent End

The status of the child
as the supreme deity
of the celestial world
is known to the crowd.
But nothing, will overcome
the anxiety of the heavens
or the thunderstorms
brewing in the night sky.
There is no solace
for the pregnant boy.

Women sit on the roof
of the outhouse.
They are blissfully ignorant
of the magical powers
of the foetus and the blood.
Bewitched by the magical herbs,
the boy disappears
into the wooded forest
in search of a violent end.
He wishes to rid himself of the shame.

But the savages
take pity on the boy
and possess him
with greater powers.
He frees himself
from the rupture
of his discontent.
Filled with helpless malice
he seeks out and exacts
vengeance upon,
the unsuspecting victims.

36. A Scatter of Bones

The magician nervously
baths in his own applause;
he feels more
than a magician
chasing a fee.
But such fickle adulation
can nourish the soul
only for a moment.

He spies himself alone
in a house of mirrors
he is a shadow of himself.
These two silhouettes meet;
in this simple act
the magician understands
the reality of his existence.
It falls upon him;
he is no more
than a scatter of bones
among
the scatters of bone.

37. Broken Images

The light
in the red rock
allows me
to see the monsters.
In the past
I have feared them
as I have feared the dust;
a handful of dust
is the distance,
between today and tomorrow.

But now,
I see their fear
and their sadness
as they carry,
their own broken images
of the shadows.

Each of us know
that regardless of our fate
and our twisted reality
that a thousand scorpions
shall fall from the sky,
and nothing,
not even the wind
can stop that from happening.

The drum beats to an imperfect time.   .
Each of us frightened of the other;
the monsters fear the monsters;
clearer signs of life, there cannot be.

38. The Rotting Corpse

Afflicted by the cruellest fate
the blind man falls into the river.
His body remains unseen, until bloated
when it tops the surface.

Released from this prison
he blasts a last glance upon the earth;
the crushing indignity of it all
overcomes his soul.

In this tumultuous state
the devil crawls across his rotting corpse,
he is wholly given over to another dimension
he is hollowed and alone.

Nothing is to be done now.
He weeps through the long nights
of radiation and pain,
defeated by the choices
he made, among the choices.

39. A Raffle for Crooked Hearts

The young shepherd is lost
in a field of red poppies;
he has led the life
of an adventurer never born.
By his own misadventure
he has fallen into outrageous fortune.
At first, it smiled upon him
now it betrays him.

He is visited by the fevered child
she is the favoured star of the grand opera.
As she lay in the field, it howls its disapproval
and the child takes up the cries of the night.
She finds the end of the labyrinth; she is safe.
The adventurer never born falls into a cycle of
    despair
and self-pity; he finds solace in the crevices of his
    own hands.
Love is a beggar's raffle for crooked hearts, he
    says.

These love notes
scribbled into the margins
of pages of lost books
will live forever;
accepting this fate
he admires
the water lily;
and wanders
among the sweet pea.

40. All Things Damned

The stones lie in peace among the stones.
They defy the aggression of the self consuming
    menaces.
They are untouchable from the other world.
They cannot be hated, harmed or harassed.
They fear the insatiable appetite of man, living for
    his own self destruction.
They lay inanimate, hidden by distraction.
They know man will damn all things.
This is the conspiracy of the stones; it lures wicked
    vices to paradise.
The rugged mountains endure to their own desire.

41. Existing in Every Cloud

Timid whispers
were shrewd enough
to give birth
to the scholars
and philosophers.
The magicians
and soothsayers;
posturing, derivative,
assured indifference
existed in every cloud;
with these impeccable skills
he walked away from his home.

The delicious panic
was not for his faint heart
but the magic credible,
more bitter than sweet.
With the intent of a man
chopping wood
he began the journey.
But, soon the appearance
of strange faces, jeering politely,
made him lose balance
and he felt lost.

In a clear running brook
he took a moment to wash away
his sins and transgressions;
the devil remained busy in the winds.

42. The Lone Adventurer

The mountain
sits gently on the head
of the screaming man.
In this captured embrace
all manner of his terrors
are peeled away and
for a moment,
insight prevails
but then,
upon further reflection;
for which, only
he is capable,
he shouts;
'my only aspiration
in life
is to be fully insured'.

In despair
the mountain replies,
'is this
the necessary proof
of your existence'.
By then,
the man has shaken free
and in his escape, he shouts,
'I will build a building
with a thousand stories'.

There is no learning
capable of devouring such thoughts,
but whether, the eyes of history

will recognise the lone adventurer
will entirely depend upon,
the success of the scheme.
Tumbling down into the river
will create only
an insolent association.
In all manner of things
lives lived
should not be gauged
by contentment.

43. By God's Lament

The stars destroy
the simple truth;
the theories of the universe
are left to the gods.
But the gods are delinquent too;
they care not for
the gift of knowledge
found in a life of books.

What good
is a collection of thoughts
they say, if man feels
no constraint by them?
This experiment of life
has simply provided,
the tools to construct
paranoia and fear.
These tortured creatures
descant at the shadows.

Knowledge is a fantasy;
a thing of magicians
it accumulates while
the fragile world crumbles.
No division will be created
by the anticipation of the future
or the opaqueness of the past.
Nothing good has come
from the casting of their minds
into the places beyond their being.
What they fear is what they are;
there is no choice in their destruction.

By the god's lament
the stones survive
to begin their work again;
human existence
contributes only
ashes to the dust.

44. Life Never Led

With no moment
in a timeless world
the fool is stalked
by the cruel glances.

Nervously, he insists upon another;
to reflect or forget
to rage or tremble
to advance his causes.

In this race against the crooked
many knowns cannot be known.
The weaving of existence
permeates the landscape
and the universe continues to expand.

The anticipated joys beckon;
a stream of water meanders
across the earth, looking for no-one,
but the silent imposition
of the living forest.

The strength of the stones;
the human capacity for kindness;
each greet in amazement,
the last stolen bewildered moments.
Fear weeps for the life never lived.

45. Every Flower is Lost

Take comfort from the familiar
the wrinkled dented features
the sagging jaw lines; the suggestion,
what we recognize
the intimacy of mortality
faces and physiques, beauty and ugliness,
each of which we are accustomed.

In our own reflection we find
the sanctity of our being
the deeply embedded trauma
of our existence, the fear
of the knowing and of the unknown.

Into these weathered old faces I dare not look
no matter how familiar each may seem to me
for each contains its own interests and self,
all human features mask deception.

Trust only the birds, the animals and plants,
the grasses, the wind and sky;
while always stubborn, known to bend
    occasionally,
they are uncompromisingly honest.

Man in the face of this drama will take no counsel.
He will seek to invade the breathing wood.
The prospect of my own body twined
with the earth will be lost forever.

Nature's point of view is carefully embedded
into every petal of every flower; but this will be
    lost to me;
lost to me because of another; and maybe
I could have found something beautiful in those
    things.

There is no doubt now that the loving shade,
will tire of this dark stupidity and
in an embrace with time, it will tire of every man.
Upon the clocks silence will settle.

46. Anxiety of the Soul

A rose loses its scent
playing among
the rusty bodies
of wrecked ships.
The state of the
crooked kingdoms
collapse once lost.
The rejected heart
is left to soften
on the corner of gin lane.
Sadness lives
among the stones.

Time is the painted enemy
but tears come all the same.
If there is a break
the living creatures
becomes the weeping souls.
Each is left to mourn
with the trees, the river
and the night sky;
existence is connected
only to the stars.

There is no god
but another set of wonders
another mystery,
it fuels the anxiety of the soul;
it drifts away
as the madness,
of each of our days
is realised.

47. Innocence

Among the silent walkers
the harvest rots in the valley;
the valley and the rivers bends.
The scarlet soldiers shift,
and take aim at the blue crane;
they hunger for the sorrow.

When you are a guilt ridden man
no amount of innocence can live
without fear of the dying days.
As he moves among the memories
the filth and the dust, he longs
for his corruptible existence.
As the moon looks upon it
it weeps a storm of tears
in the silent corner.
This news proves there exists
in this world of caves, no cave
to hide from the excesses of our days.

In deference to it all, bleakly
futile death puts down his book,
and life lays down to rest.
In among the innocence
the shameful loss
is keenly felt
and keenly lived.

48. A Chorus for the Damned

Never shall
a greater waste lie
than among
the retreat from the sea.
Of the dead
there is no fortune
to be told;
each is dead.

Laid to their restless end
the energy of their bodies
are now forces upon the paranoid mind.
Time accepts no humour
for the waste, for the
withered breath, and stays silent,
wisely silent.

The sunshine arrives
at the crossroads.
The mind, left alone
fills with monsters
and blames the stones
for the dead.
The product of indifferent grief
makes enemies of the stones.
The myth of being transcends
into the knowing of a foe.

Consumed and paralysed
all fear takes charge;
it howls a chorus for the damned.
These ruinous lies
beget a parting gift;
its resources malign the living;
a rose without scent
a daisy bereft of petals
and a sunflower
as black as night;
mistrust guides mistrust.

49. To God I defer the Dead

Death does not touch me
and I take no responsibility
for the dead.
The leaves decay,
this is their want,
the striking note
is the maker
of its own destruction;
it hangs
for a delicate moment.
The dead are lost
to their own moments;
some desperately missed
some fondly remembered,
all sweetly timed.
I take no responsibility
for the dead;
I do not keep them
to their ordinary ways.

Infamy and grief
may transcend their time
but no learning
can come from the past.
The historic
simply distracts
my focus from
my own culpability;
I will only grieve
who I have known.
To god I defer our dead
to do unto them
as he sees fit.

With him they exist
in another
kind of dimension
safe and happy
are their souls
but for their sins.

It becomes
unimportant that in life
they were abused
moulded into ghastly shapes
defiled from the first moments
of their laughing day
until they existed only
as blemishes
on the moonlight.

In life I was taught a few things,
and a few things, only.
As a man, I was taught to be strong,
as a woman, I was taught to be pretty.
Without strength or beauty
I was taught to be powerless.
The limping devil experienced my will
and claimed power over my existence.

In my shameful exclusion from life,
despite living, I was made to bear
my rejected possibilities.
All self knowledge tempts
the deserted mind into envy.
To me, for all I was offered
in the valley of the thieves
I felt only a stolen river
could in the end, beg for nothing
but a dead silent dream.

50. The Desires

The uttered scorn
glances sideways
and seeks to move the oceans.
It is through the ears of these men
the anxious music passes
the tempo of every shade
cuts across the score
its mishaps survive
its genius mimes;
and forgiven
are the works unplayed.

This wasted course
despoils the rose
and corrupts the prose;
leaving me
to wish for the desires of the dead
to cast off this villain
to exclude it from this violent play
which endures forever,
without interval.

But I know
regardless of the script written
the morning will not say
what the storm did
it will only quietly point
to the actions done.

For sixty years now
I have resisted this temptation,
I have quietly listened,
sat speechless,
not reacted to these panicked faces,
remained inactive to their baseness,
in fear of the blooded corpse
and I am left now
only to count my crimes.
Vanity abuses
each greatness made.

51. My Actions my Own

A thought enters his mind;
from the hour of my death
I shall be wholly of the gods
free of the will of other man;
no longer can they make obstacles
no longer can they instil fear
in me; from that time my actions
and my life will be to me.
There are no constraints
in the afterlife; he embraces the bliss.
Such man no longer grips the soil
or breathes the air. His soul is not subject
to the nature of other men; the purple
becomes the red and is the yellow.

52. Drop Velvet in Every Scene

The making of clouds
was an art that
had been handed down
from father to son
from mother to daughter
for nine generations.
It had never been perfected
and the unsolved mysteries
remained unresolved.

On this day
the ancient ceiling panels
were being laid out on the floor.
These old works
captured an amazing beauty.
These were collected
in the decoration of the mountains
and the gardens.
They lay far below the clouds.

Thirty three people
had worked for a year
to create the eight
delicate masterpieces.
Each cloud hung
like drop velvet in every scene
each one was a privilege
for the emperor to behold;
yet today, on this day,
the view embraced
paid homage to
the embroiderers and
the fabric makers.

Many of these ancient traditions
had been lost for
a thousand years now.
The last vestiges
of the talents
were used to respond
to modern tastes.
These were far removed
from the skills
of the traditional southern tribes.

53. My Memory of Life

I am very aware of dying.
I know I will be a memory soon.
It has always been a dilemma for me.
I think the hardship of taking care of me,
or loving me, has been my obsession with death.
It has made me invest in people forever.

Life is strange.
As you reach its end, you realize
that so much has gone by,
so much more is left to do,
so little has been done.
I wanted to write so simple
and so short a story,
a work of art.
I never can satisfy that need
that lives within me
to achieve something
of incredible height.
It troubles me deeply.

Do I find joy in life?
I cannot help remember
that a great man,
after a life of gruffness,
but with the solace
of being the maker of beautiful things,
asked at the end of his life,
is this it?
I am also left to ask,
is this it?
It really hurts me
to think that this was his last question.

He had worked so hard throughout his life
and in the end,
all that was left
was what he did.
I realize there are no guarantees
to be remembered forever.
To think it possible, that is vanity.

They will all forget
the day after you are dead
that you are dead,
the day after that, I suppose,
you won't even be doubly dead,
for all that might be worth.
We could all ask,
why bother being born at all?
I suppose I did not make that choice.
But to live, for me,
that was a joy;
it was a great joy.
To be able to have friends
was my greatest joy;
it would have been a terrible loss for me
not to know my friends.
Also, I think good books
are a delight of life;
it is a magic time to be able to make one;
it is in those times,
that all else,
fades away.

You know,
in spite of any protests
I do everything I want to do.
I am a lucky man,
I feel, I smell, I look,
I taste, I breathe;
But, I am not earth shatteringly important.
I am not better
than anyone else, maybe only,
that I can claim
to have always been
most honest.
I am good with children
but that is because I don't believe in children;
I just tell them about things
in the way I tell all things
about things;
a taste of joy is an innocent mind.

54. In the Robber's Bones

For all my temptations
do not presume who I am
or seek to delay my parody;
I will not be held
to these ordinary ways,
for me, each moment
can recommend the next.

The difference
between hunger and love
survives in the misfortune
that lies between blame
and the weather.
Without permission
the fears can intersect
and my sad envies
can deny the chaotic gods.

My existence can proceed,
at whatever, odd pace,
the grace of the universe decides.
It can decide if it does,
whether the innocent bride,
should hang from the gallows
in the robber's bones.

If upon my passing
I am a shallow hollow man,
without delight or touch,
the inconstancy of my flesh
can deliver order to my vessel,
and my bones, in a million years,
can join the stones; the beast
that repeats itself.
At that time, my perfect identity,
no doubt, can make argument
for its own cause.

Wakefield Press is an independent publishing and
distribution company based in Adelaide, South Australia.
We love good stories and publish beautiful books.
To see our full range of books, please visit our website at
www.wakefieldpress.com.au
where all titles are available for purchase.

Find us!

Twitter: www.twitter.com/wakefieldpress
Facebook: www.facebook.com/wakefield.press
Instagram: instagram.com/wakefieldpress